AMANPREET KAUR

Attitude Revolution

Your Key to Self-Confidence and Impact

First published by Rana Books (UK, India) 2023

Copyright © 2023 by Amanpreet Kaur

All rights reserved. No part of this publication may be reproduced, stored or transmitted in any form or by any means, electronic, mechanical, photocopying, recording, scanning, or otherwise without written permission from the publisher. It is illegal to copy this book, post it to a website, or distribute it by any other means without permission.

First edition

Contents

1	Understanding Attitude for Girls	1
2	Why Girls Should Have Attitude	7
3	Developing a Positive Attitude	10
4	Expressing Attitude Effectively	14
5	Avoiding Negative Attitudes	21
6	Nurturing Healthy Relationships	26
7	Overcoming Challenges and Adversity	30
8	Embracing Individuality	36
9	Empowering Others	40
10	Balancing Attitude with Kindness	44
11	Thriving in a Male-Dominated World	48
12	Embracing Success with Attitude	52

1

Understanding Attitude for Girls

Attitude plays a significant role in shaping an individual's thoughts actions and overall behavior. It is a reflection of one's mindset feelings beliefs and values. Attitude influences how a person perceives and responds to the world around them. In the context of girls understanding attitude becomes crucial as it affects their self-perception confidence and social interactions. This article aims to provide a deep understanding of attitude for girls including its definition importance and various types supplemented with relevant examples.

Definition of Attitude:

Attitude refers to a person's predisposition to respond cither positively or negatively to people objects situations or ideas. It is a psychological construct that forms an individual's evaluation affective reaction and behavioral tendencies towards various aspects of life. Attitude is shaped by a combination of cognitive affective and behavioral components. In essence it is the lens through which girls perceive and interpret the world influencing their thoughts decisions and actions.

Importance of Attitude:

Attitude holds immense significance in a girl's life due to its powerful impact on various aspects of her personal and interpersonal growth. Some key reasons why understanding attitude is crucial for girls are:

1. Self-Perception and Confidence: Attitude profoundly influences how girls perceive themselves. Positive attitudes such as self-acceptance self-belief and self-worth build healthy self-esteem and confidence. Conversely negative attitudes can hinder personal growth and diminish self-confidence. Understanding and cultivating a positive attitude can empower girls to have a strong sense of self and face life's challenges with resilience.

Example: Jane a teenage girl has a positive attitude towards her abilities and strengths. She believes in her potential and chooses to take up challenging tasks. This attitude fuels her confidence and helps her excel in academics sports and other endeavors.

2. Emotional Well-Being: Attitude greatly impacts emotional well-being. A positive attitude fosters optimism resilience and emotional stability enabling girls to cope with stress setbacks and emotional challenges effectively. On the other hand a negative attitude characterized by pessimism and self-doubt can lead to anxiety depression and low emotional well-being.

Example: Sarah faces a series of rejections while applying for college scholarships. Instead of becoming disheartened she maintains a positive attitude perceiving the rejections as opportunities to learn and improve. This attitude helps her stay motivated and emotionally balanced throughout the process.

3. Interpersonal Relationships: Attitude significantly affects how girls interact with others. A positive attitude promotes empathy understanding assertiveness and effective communication leading to healthy and fulfilling relationships. Conversely negative attitudes like prejudice arrogance or a defensive mindset can strain relationships and hinder personal growth.

Example: Emily has a positive attitude towards people from different cultures and backgrounds. She treats everyone with respect and seeks to understand their perspectives. This attitude fosters strong connections and enriches her relationships both personally and professionally.

4. Personal Growth and Success: Attitude plays a vital role in personal growth and achieving success. A growth-oriented attitude characterized by a willingness to learn adapt and embrace challenges drives continuous improvement and empowers girls to reach their full potential. A fixed mindset attitude limits growth and hampers success.

Example: Mia faces a setback in her career when her business idea fails. Instead of giving up she adopts a growth mindset attitude. She identifies her mistakes learns from them and redirects her efforts towards a new venture. This attitude enables her to bounce back and achieve long-term success.

Types of Attitude:

Attitudes can be classified into several types based on different dimensions. While there are various categorizations this article highlights four prominent types of attitudes specifically relevant for girls:

1. Positive Attitude: A positive attitude reflects optimism confidence and a hopeful outlook towards life. It involves perceiving opportunities focusing on strengths and being grateful for blessings. A positive attitude helps girls build resilience cope with challenges and maintain overall well-being.

Example: Sophia faces a challenging situation at school. Instead of feeling overwhelmed she maintains a positive attitude focusing on finding solutions rather than dwelling on the problem. This attitude helps her overcome obstacles with ease.

2. Negative Attitude: A negative attitude is characterized by pessimism pessimism and a tendency to focus on flaws and problems. It involves self-doubt a fear of failure and a belief that things will go wrong. Negative attitudes hinder personal growth erode self-confidence and strain relationships.

Example: Lisa constantly doubts her abilities and believes she will never succeed. As a result she rarely attempts new challenges fearing failure. This negative attitude holds her back from exploring her full potential.

3. Assertive Attitude: An assertive attitude reflects confidence self-assuredness and the ability to express opinions needs and

desires in a respectful manner. It involves communicating effectively setting boundaries and standing up for oneself while considering others' perspectives. An assertive attitude helps girls develop healthy relationships and maintain self-respect.

Example: Rebecca confidently expresses her opinions in team discussions engaging in constructive debates while respecting others' viewpoints. This assertive attitude enables her to be an effective team player and contribute to meaningful collaborations.

4. Growth Mindset Attitude: A growth mindset attitude involves a belief in the ability to develop skills intelligence and talents through effort and perseverance. It fosters a love for learning embraces challenges and sees failures as opportunities for growth. A growth mindset attitude encourages girls to reach beyond their comfort zones and cultivate lifelong learning.

Example: Lily regularly seeks feedback from her teachers and peers to identify areas for improvement. She believes that with enough practice and effort she can develop her skills and excel in any field. This growth mindset attitude propels her towards continuous learning and personal growth.

Conclusion:

Understanding attitude is crucial for girls as it shapes their self-perception confidence emotional well-being relationships and overall personal growth. Positive attitudes empower girls to navigate life's challenges with resilience embrace opportunities and achieve success. Conversely negative attitudes limit their potential and hinder personal progress. By developing positive attitudes such as optimism assertiveness and a growth mindset girls can cultivate a strong sense of self build healthy relationships and unlock their full potential.

2

Why Girls Should Have Attitude

Attitude is often associated with a negative connotation implying arrogance or rudeness. However in this context we are referring to attitude as a positive attribute that girls should embrace. Having attitude encompasses empowerment self-confidence setting boundaries dealing with stereotypes and societal expectations and enhancing leadership skills. This article will explore these aspects in depth providing examples along the way.

1. Empowerment and Self-Confidence:
   Having attitude allows girls to feel empowered and confident in themselves. It is vital for girls to have a strong sense of self-worth and belief in their abilities. By embracing attitude girls can assert their own power and pursue their dreams fearlessly.

For example a girl with attitude might stand up for herself when faced with discrimination or inequality. She might assert her rights and demand the same opportunities as her male counterparts. This attitude empowers her to break barriers and excel in various domains including education career and personal life.

2. Setting Boundaries:

Attitude enables girls to set boundaries and refuse to tolerate mistreatment or disrespect. It encourages them to stand up for themselves and assert their needs and desires. It is essential for girls to learn how to say "no" and establish healthy boundaries in all aspects of life.

For instance a girl with attitude may refuse to engage in activities that compromise her values or personal well-being. She understands the importance of self-care mental health and personal integrity. This attitude helps her navigate relationships friendships and social interactions with confidence and self-respect.

3. Dealing with Stereotypes and Societal Expectations:

Girls are often subjected to stereotypes and societal expectations that limit their potential and restrict their choices. Having attitude allows girls to challenge these stereotypes and break free from societal norms. It encourages them to live life on their terms and pursue their passions regardless of societal pressures.

For example a girl with attitude might choose to pursue a career in a male-dominated field challenging the notion that certain professions are only for men. She might reject beauty standards or traditional gender roles embracing her true self and celebrating her uniqueness. This attitude helps girls redefine societal norms and pave the way for future generations.

4. Enhancing Leadership Skills:

Attitude plays a crucial role in enhancing leadership skills among girls. It instills qualities like assertiveness resilience and the ability to influence others positively. Girls with attitude are not afraid to take charge make decisions and lead by example.

For instance a girl with attitude might take the lead in group projects inspiring others to follow her lead. She may initiate social change or advocate for important causes mobilizing communities and making a significant impact. This attitude helps girls develop crucial leadership skills that are important in all aspects of life whether it be school work or personal relationships.

In conclusion having attitude is essential for girls as it empowers them builds self-confidence enables them to set boundaries challenges stereotypes and enhances leadership skills. Girls who embrace attitude are more likely to believe in themselves stand up for their rights and pursue their passions with determination. They become agents of change and instrumental in breaking societal barriers and reshaping the world around them. It is crucial to encourage and support girls in developing a positive attitude that empowers them to become strong independent individuals who can overcome any challenge and achieve their goals.

3

Developing a Positive Attitude

Developing a positive attitude is crucial for personal growth resilience and overall well-being. It involves the ability to approach life with optimism maintain a constructive outlook and respond to challenges in a healthy manner. In this section we will delve deeper into various aspects of developing a positive attitude including self-reflection and awareness building self-esteem cultivating a growth mindset and practicing self-care and mental health.

1. Self-Reflection and Awareness

Self-reflection and self-awareness are fundamental building blocks of developing a positive attitude. It involves taking the time to understand oneself including strengths weaknesses values and beliefs. By becoming more aware of our thoughts emotions and behaviors we gain valuable insights into how they impact our attitude and overall well-being.

Self-reflection can be practiced through journaling meditation or engaging in introspective exercises. By reflecting on our experiences we can identify patterns learn from past mistakes and make conscious choices to improve our attitude. For example if we notice that we often respond to challenges with negativity or self-doubt we can develop strategies to reframe our perspective and approach things with a more positive mindset.

2. Building Self-Esteem

Building self-esteem is vital for developing a positive attitude. Self-esteem refers to the overall sense of self-worth and confidence that individuals have in themselves. When we have a healthy level of self-esteem we are more likely to have a positive outlook on life and a greater belief in our ability to overcome challenges.

There are several strategies to build self-esteem such as practicing self-acceptance and self-compassion setting realistic goals celebrating achievements and surrounding ourselves with positive and supportive people. It's important to challenge negative self-talk and replace it with positive affirmations. For instance instead of thinking "I will never be good enough we can reframe it to "I am capable and deserving of success."

3. Cultivating a Growth Mindset

A growth mindset is the belief that our abilities and intelligence can be developed through dedication and effort. Individuals with a growth mindset embrace challenges see failures as opportunities for learning and are motivated to improve themselves continuously. Cultivating a growth mindset is central to developing a positive attitude as it promotes resilience perseverance and a willingness to take risks.

To develop a growth mindset it's essential to embrace the learning process and view setbacks as valuable lessons. Regularly seeking out new challenges engaging in continuous learning and seeking feedback are ways to foster a growth mindset. For example instead of feeling discouraged by a setback individuals with a growth mindset would analyze what went wrong learn from it and adjust their approach accordingly.

4. Practicing Self-Care and Mental Health

Taking care of our mental and emotional well-being is a critical component of developing a positive attitude. When we neglect our self-care stress negativity and burnout can take a toll on our overall attitude. Prioritizing self-care activities is essential for maintaining a positive mindset.

Self-care encompasses various activities that nurture our mental emotional and physical well-being. It can include activities such as exercising regularly getting enough sleep practicing mindfulness and relaxation techniques engaging in hobbies or activities that bring joy and establishing healthy boundaries in relationships. By carving out time for self-care individuals can recharge reduce stress levels and improve their overall attitude.

In conclusion developing a positive attitude involves several interconnected aspects. Self-reflection and awareness allow individuals to understand their thoughts emotions and behaviors and make conscious choices to improve their attitude. Building self-esteem provides a foundation for a positive outlook and belief in oneself. Cultivating a growth mindset fosters resilience motivation and adaptability. Lastly practicing self-care and prioritizing mental health is crucial for maintaining a positive attitude and overall well-being.

By embracing these principles and actively working towards developing a positive attitude individuals can enhance their personal growth increase their resilience in the face of challenges and improve their overall quality of life. It is an ongoing process that requires dedication self-compassion and a willingness to change. With persistence and the right tools anyone can cultivate a positive attitude and reap the benefits it brings.

4

Expressing Attitude Effectively

Expressing attitude effectively involves effectively communicating your thoughts opinions and emotions in a respectful and assertive manner. It is essential to develop good communication skills understand body language and non-verbal cues learn how to handle conflict and criticism and balance firmness with respect. In this article we will explore each of these aspects in-depth provide examples and discuss how they contribute to effective attitude expression.

1. Assertiveness and Communication Skills:

Assertiveness is the ability to express your thoughts feelings and desires in a clear and confident manner while respecting the rights and opinions of others. Effective communication is crucial for demonstrating assertiveness. Here are some key elements of assertive communication:

- Clear Expression: Assertiveness involves expressing your ideas and needs clearly avoiding ambiguity or passive-aggressive behavior. For example instead of saying "I guess it's fine assertively state "I appreciate your suggestion but I have a different perspective."

- Active Listening: Actively listen to others' perspectives showing genuine interest and empathy. Paying attention nodding and maintaining eye contact are essential non-verbal cues that demonstrate active listening.

- Using "I" Statements: Use "I" statements to express how you feel or what you think about a situation. This approach takes ownership of your emotions and avoids blaming others. For example say "I feel disappointed when I am not included in the decision-making process rather than "You always make decisions without considering me."

- Setting Boundaries: Assertiveness also involves setting clear boundaries and expressing them respectfully. For instance saying "I understand you need my help but I have other commitments at the moment. I will be available later helps establish boundaries without being aggressive or passive.

2. Body Language and Non-Verbal Cues:

Body language and non-verbal cues play a significant role in expressing attitude effectively. The way we stand gesture and maintain eye contact can communicate a range of emotions and attitudes. Understanding and utilizing these non-verbal cues can help enhance effective communication. Here are some key elements to consider:

- Posture and Stance: Standing or sitting upright with an open posture communicates confidence and attentiveness. Slouching or crossing arms may convey defensiveness or disinterest.

- Eye Contact: Maintaining appropriate eye contact shows respect and engagement in the conversation. However excessive or intense eye contact might come across as aggressive. It is important to find a balance.

- Facial Expressions: Facial expressions are powerful indicators of emotions and attitudes. Smiling nodding and using appropriate facial expressions help convey interest and understanding.

- Hand Gestures: Appropriate hand gestures can reinforce your verbal message and make it more engaging. However excessive or inappropriate gestures can distract or confuse the listener.

- Voice Tone and Pace: The tone and pace of your voice can influence how your attitude is perceived. Speaking with a calm and confident tone and avoiding mumbling or speaking too fast can enhance effective communication.

3. Handling Conflict and Criticism:

Conflict and criticism are inevitable in both personal and professional settings. Efficiently managing these situations is crucial for expressing attitude effectively. Here are some strategies to handle conflict and criticism constructively:

- Remain Calm: When faced with conflict or criticism it is

important to remain calm and composed. Take a moment to collect your thoughts before responding. Reacting impulsively can lead to further escalation.

- Active Listening and Empathy: Actively listen to the other person's perspective without interrupting. Try to understand their point of view and empathize with their concerns. This helps establish a respectful dialogue.

- Use "I" Statements: Express your feelings and thoughts using "I" statements rather than attacking or blaming the other person. This approach encourages open communication and helps avoid defensiveness.

- Seek Common Ground: Find areas of agreement or shared interests to build upon. Focusing on common goals can help in finding solutions and resolving conflicts more effectively.

- Collaborative Problem-Solving: Instead of focusing on winning or being right adopt a collaborative approach to find mutually beneficial solutions. This encourages a positive attitude and fosters open communication.

4. Balancing Firmness with Respect:

Expressing attitude effectively involves finding a balance between being firm in your convictions and opinions while still demonstrating respect for others. Here are some key considerations:

- Confidence and Conviction: It is important to express your opinions ideas and values confidently. Being firm in your beliefs shows authenticity and conviction.

- Respectful Language: Even when disagreeing it is crucial to use respectful and appropriate language. Avoid personal attacks derogatory remarks or offensive language that can harm relationships and hinder effective communication.

- Active Listening and Validation: Actively listen to others' points of view even if you disagree. Validate their perspectives and show respect for their opinions. This helps foster a harmonious atmosphere where differing opinions can be explored without animosity.

- Flexibility and Openness: While staying firm on important principles it is also necessary to stay open to new ideas perspectives and feedback. Being flexible in your thinking encourages growth and collaboration.

- Constructive Feedback: Provide feedback in a constructive manner focusing on specific behaviors or actions rather than attacking personal characteristics. This helps to maintain respect while addressing areas of improvement.

To illustrate the above concepts let's consider an example:

John is a team leader in a marketing firm. During a team meeting he notices that some team members are constantly interrupting others and not allowing them to express their ideas. John understands the importance of expressing attitude effectively and decides to address this issue. He starts by using assertive communication skills:

John: "I've noticed that there seems to be a lot of interruption during our meetings and some team members are not getting a chance to share their ideas. I believe it's important that everyone has an opportunity to be heard."

Next John pays attention to his body language and non-verbal cues. He maintains a confident posture maintains eye contact and uses appropriate facial expressions to convey his engagement. While addressing the issue John remains calm and composed actively listening to his team members' responses:

John: "I would like to hear from each team member without any interruption. Let's practice active listening and allow each person to complete their thoughts before discussing further."

John demonstrates his ability to handle conflict and criticism by addressing the issue directly but respectfully. He seeks common ground by acknowledging the importance of everyone's opinions and fostering a collaborative problem-solving approach:

John: "I understand that we all have valuable insights to share. By actively listening and respecting each other's ideas we can create a more inclusive and productive team environment."

Throughout the process John balances firmness with respect. He expresses his concerns assertively maintains a strong stance on the importance of effective communication and encourages his team members to adopt a more respectful attitude without demeaning anyone:

John: "Let's strive for a balance between expressing our thoughts assertively and creating room for others to do the same. We can create a positive team atmosphere by encouraging open dialogue while respecting each other's perspectives."

In this example John effectively applies the principles of expressing attitude effectively by using assertiveness and communication skills understanding body language and non-verbal cues handling conflict and criticism constructively and balancing firmness with respect.

In conclusion expressing attitude effectively is crucial for effective communication. By developing assertiveness and communication skills understanding body language and non-verbal cues handling conflict and criticism constructively and balancing firmness with respect individuals can communicate their thoughts opinions and emotions in a respectful and assertive manner. Mastering these skills is a continuous process but by putting these principles into practice individuals can enhance their ability to express their attitudes effectively in various personal and professional contexts.

5

Avoiding Negative Attitudes

Maintaining a positive and healthy mindset is crucial for personal growth building strong relationships and achieving success in various aspects of life. Negative attitudes such as toxicity manipulation arrogance entitlement aggression rudeness closed-mindedness and judgmental behavior not only harm our mental well-being but also impact our interactions with others. In this guide we will delve deeper into each of these negative attitudes exploring their effects and providing examples to better understand how to avoid them.

1. Toxicity and Manipulation:
Toxicity refers to behaviors attitudes or actions that are harmful draining or detrimental to individuals or the environment. Manipulation on the other hand involves influencing or controlling others for personal gain often without their awareness or consent. These negative attitudes can poison relationships create conflicts and hinder personal growth.

Example:

Imagine a work environment where one colleague consistently spreads rumors gossips about others and undermines their colleagues' efforts to achieve success. This toxic behavior can result in a tense atmosphere decreased productivity and damaged relationships between colleagues.

To avoid toxicity and manipulation:

a. Foster open and honest communication: Encourage transparent communication within your personal and professional relationships. This promotes trust respect and cooperation while discouraging toxic behaviors.

b. Set boundaries: Recognize and establish appropriate boundaries to protect yourself from toxic or manipulative individuals. This may involve limiting your exposure to toxic influences or confronting manipulation when it occurs.

c. Practice self-care: Prioritize self-care by engaging in activities that promote mental and emotional well-being such as exercise mindfulness or spending time with loved ones. Taking care of yourself helps build resilience against toxic attitudes.

2. Arrogance and Entitlement:

Arrogance and entitlement are negative attitudes characterized by an exaggerated sense of superiority self-importance and self-centeredness. Individuals with these attitudes often disregard others' feelings perspectives and contributions leading to strained relationships and lack of collaboration.

Example:

Consider a situation in which a student believes they are inherently smarter than their classmates dismissing their peers' opinions and refusing to engage in group work. Such arrogance and entitlement hinder teamwork impede knowledge-sharing and create a hostile learning environment.

To avoid arrogance and entitlement:

a. Practice humility: Recognize that everyone has their own unique strengths and no one is superior in every aspect. Cultivate humility by acknowledging and appreciating the talents and capabilities of others.

b. Foster empathy: Put yourself in the shoes of others to better understand their perspectives and experiences. Developing empathy promotes understanding compassion and a sense of equality.

c. Encourage diversity and collaboration: Embrace diverse perspectives and actively collaborate with others. By valuing different viewpoints and working together you can create an inclusive environment that fosters growth and innovation.

3. Aggression and Rudeness:

Aggression and rudeness involve displaying hostile ill-mannered or disrespectful behavior toward others. Such negative attitudes can create tension destroy relationships and hinder effective communication.

Example:

Imagine a customer service representative who responds aggressively to customer complaints using harsh language and belittling customers instead of listening and finding a solution. This aggressive and rude behavior escalates tensions damages customer satisfaction and harms the company's reputation.

To avoid aggression and rudeness:

a. Practice active listening: Give others your full attention take their concerns seriously and respond with empathy and understanding. Being mindful of your communication can help avoid aggressive or rude reactions.

b. Develop emotional intelligence: Cultivate self-awareness emotional regulation and empathy to better manage your emotions and respond to others in a more constructive and respectful manner.

c. Seek constructive feedback: Actively seek feedback from peers colleagues or trusted individuals to identify areas where you may come across as aggressive or rude. This feedback can help you identify triggers and develop strategies for improvement.

4. Closed-Mindedness and Judgmental Behavior:

Closed-mindedness involves having a narrow perspective rejecting new ideas or alternative viewpoints and being resistant to change. Judgmental behavior on the other hand entails forming hasty opinions about others without fully understanding their backgrounds or situations. These negative attitudes hinder personal growth limit our ability to collaborate and impair our understanding of the world.

Example:

Consider a scenario where a person refuses to accept ideas or beliefs that differ from their own dismissing any opposing viewpoints as invalid without substantial consideration. This closed-minded attitude stunts personal growth inhibits learning and creates a rift between individuals.

To avoid closed-mindedness and judgmental behavior:

a. Cultivate open-mindedness: Approach new ideas with curiosity and a willingness to learn. Embrace diverse perspectives and actively seek out new information to broaden your understanding.

b. Practice empathy and tolerance: Suspend judgment and try to understand others' perspectives even if they differ from your own. Recognize that individuals may have different experiences and knowledge that contribute to their viewpoints.

c. Challenge your biases: Reflect on your own biases and prejudices and actively challenge them. Engage in dialogue with individuals from different backgrounds read diverse literature and expose yourself to contrasting viewpoints. This helps broaden your mindset and increase tolerance.

In conclusion avoiding negative attitudes is essential for personal growth maintaining healthy relationships and fostering a positive environment. By actively recognizing and addressing toxic behaviors arrogance aggression closed-mindedness and judgmental tendencies individuals can promote harmonious interactions and create a nurturing space for personal and collective development. Developing self-awareness practicing empathy and fostering a mindset of openness and respect are key steps in cultivating positive attitudes and building a more inclusive and supportive society.

6

Nurturing Healthy Relationships

Nurturing healthy relationships is crucial for our overall well-being and happiness. Whether it's our relationships with family friends colleagues or romantic partners a strong and healthy bond can bring us the support joy and fulfillment we need in our lives. In this article we will explore the key elements that contribute to building and nurturing healthy relationships including developing mutual respect trust and honesty supporting and uplifting others and encouraging collaboration and teamwork. Examples will be provided to illustrate these concepts in action.

1. Developing Mutual Respect:

Respect forms the foundation of any healthy relationship. It involves acknowledging valuing and appreciating the thoughts feelings and boundaries of others. When we develop mutual respect we create an environment of openness and acceptance which fosters trust and emotional safety.

Example: In a romantic relationship partners should respect

each other's personal space and opinions. They should actively listen to each other and never dismiss or demean each other's thoughts or feelings. This mutual respect creates a strong foundation for a healthy and harmonious partnership.

2. Trust and Honesty:

Trust and honesty are essential components of healthy relationships. Trust is built over time through consistent and reliable behavior whereas honesty is the willingness to be open sincere and transparent about our thoughts feelings and actions. When trust and honesty are present the relationship becomes more secure intimate and resilient.

Example: In a friendship trust is demonstrated when friends confide in each other keep each other's secrets and support one another in times of need. Honesty is shown when friends openly communicate their feelings or concerns even if it might be uncomfortable thus building a deeper level of trust and understanding.

3. Supporting and Uplifting Others:

Supporting and uplifting others is a vital aspect of nurturing healthy relationships. It involves being there for the people we care about helping them overcome challenges and celebrating their successes. By offering emotional support and encouragement we create a sense of belonging and strengthen our connections with others.

Example: In a family setting supporting and uplifting others can be shown by parents actively participating in their children's interests attending their performances or games and offering words of encouragement. This support helps children develop self-confidence resilience and a sense of belonging within their family unit.

4. Encouraging Collaboration and Teamwork:
Collaboration and teamwork are crucial in both personal and professional relationships. When we work together towards a common goal we foster a sense of unity mutual understanding and shared responsibility. This not only strengthens our relationships but also helps us achieve greater success and fulfillment.

Example: In a work environment encouraging collaboration and teamwork can involve fostering open communication respecting diverse opinions and promoting a culture of mutual support. By working together on projects and pooling their individual strengths colleagues can achieve better results and build stronger working relationships.

Building and nurturing healthy relationships require ongoing effort patience and understanding. It's important to remember that no relationship is perfect and conflicts and disagreements may arise. However by incorporating the aforementioned elements into our relationships we can create a strong foundation that helps us navigate challenges and cultivate strong bonds.

In conclusion nurturing healthy relationships involves developing mutual respect trust and honesty supporting and uplifting others and encouraging collaboration and teamwork. These elements contribute to the foundation of strong and fulfilling connections with our loved ones friends colleagues and partners. By actively practicing these principles we can create a positive and supportive environment that enhances our overall well-being and happiness.

7

Overcoming Challenges and Adversity

Overcoming challenges and adversity. In life we often encounter obstacles that can be challenging and even overwhelming at times. However it is important to develop strategies and attitudes that can help us overcome these challenges and grow stronger as a result. In this discussion we will explore four key aspects of overcoming challenges and adversity: building resilience cultivating positive thinking and optimism seeking help and support and embracing failure and learning from mistakes.

1. Building Resilience:
   Resilience can be defined as the ability to bounce back from difficult experiences and adapt to new circumstances. Building resilience is crucial in overcoming challenges and adversity. It involves developing the mental and emotional strength to face challenges head-on and persevere through adversity. Here are some strategies to build resilience:

a. Acceptance: Acknowledging that challenges are a part of

life and accepting them as opportunities for growth can help develop resilience. Instead of viewing challenges as roadblocks see them as stepping stones towards personal development.

b. Self-Reflection: Take the time to reflect on past experiences and identify the lessons learned. This self-reflection can help build resilience by understanding how you have overcome challenges in the past and applying those strategies to current situations.

c. Self-Care: Taking care of yourself physically emotionally and mentally is essential for building resilience. Engage in activities that bring you joy and relaxation such as exercise meditation spending time with loved ones or pursuing hobbies.

d. Flexibility: Being flexible and adaptable in the face of challenges is key to building resilience. Learn to adjust your expectations and plans when necessary and approach obstacles with an open mind.

2. Positive Thinking and Optimism:

Positive thinking and optimism play a crucial role in overcoming challenges and adversity. They can help shift your mindset from a place of despair and hopelessness to a mindset of possibility and opportunity. Here's how you can cultivate positive thinking and optimism:

a. Reframing: Challenge negative thoughts and reframe them into more positive and empowering ones. For example instead of saying "I can't do this replace it with "I can learn and grow from this experience."

b. Gratitude: Cultivate a sense of gratitude for the things you have in your life. Focusing on the positives can help shift your perspective and foster optimism.

c. Visualization: Visualize yourself successfully overcoming the challenges you are facing. This positive imagery can help boost your confidence and motivation.

d. Surrounding Yourself with Positivity: Surround yourself with positive people and environments that uplift and inspire you. Their optimism and support can help you navigate challenges more effectively.

3. Seeking Help and Support:

Facing challenges alone can be overwhelming. Seeking help and support from others is a crucial aspect of overcoming adversity. Here are some ways to seek help and support:

a. Reach out to Friends and Family: Lean on your loved ones for emotional support. Share your challenges and concerns with them and ask for their advice and perspectives.

b. Seek Professional Help: When facing significant challenges professional guidance can be beneficial. Consider reaching out to therapists coaches or mentors who can provide valuable insights and strategies.

c. Join Support Groups: Joining support groups or communities with individuals who have faced similar challenges can provide a sense of belonging and understanding. It can also offer practical advice and encouragement.

d. Collaborate with Others: When facing complex challenges consider collaborating with others who have the expertise or experience that can contribute to finding solutions. Collaborative efforts often lead to better outcomes.

4. Embracing Failure and Learning from Mistakes:

Failure and mistakes are inevitable aspects of life. However how we respond to them can determine our ability to overcome challenges and grow. Here's how you can embrace failure and learn from mistakes:

a. Shift Your Perspective: View failures as opportunities for growth and learning rather than personal shortcomings. Recognize that failure is a natural part of the learning process.

b. Analyze and Reflect: Take the time to reflect on your failures and mistakes. Identify what went wrong and evaluate what you can learn from the experience. This self-reflection can help you avoid similar mistakes in the future.

c. Adjust and Adapt: Use the lessons learned from failures and mistakes to make necessary adjustments and adaptations. Apply the new knowledge to improve your strategies and approaches in future endeavors.

d. Perseverance: Embracing failure requires perseverance and resilience. Don't let setbacks discourage you or hinder your progress. Stay focused on your goals and keep pushing forward.

To illustrate these concepts let's consider an example. Imagine a student who is preparing for a challenging exam. They face various obstacles such as a heavy workload limited time for preparation and self-doubt. To overcome these challenges and adversity the student can apply the strategies discussed:

- Building Resilience: The student can accept that the exam is a challenging task reflect on past successes practice self-care by managing their stress and remain flexible in their study plan.

- Positive Thinking and Optimism: The student can reframe negative thoughts about the difficulty of the exam into positive ones express gratitude for the opportunity to learn and grow visualize success in the exam and surround themselves with supportive peers who share a positive outlook.

- Seeking Help and Support: The student can seek help from classmates discuss challenging concepts with their professors join a study group or online forum for assistance and consult a tutor or academic advisor.

- Embracing Failure and Learning from Mistakes: If the student faces setbacks such as lower-than-expected grades on practice exams they can shift their perspective analyze their mistakes adjust their study strategies and persevere in their preparation.

By utilizing these strategies the student can effectively overcome challenges and adversity ultimately achieving success in their exam.

In conclusion overcoming challenges and adversity is an essential part of personal growth and development. Building resilience cultivating positive thinking and optimism seeking help and support and embracing failure and learning from mistakes are key strategies to navigate through challenging situations. By applying these approaches in different areas of life individuals can develop the skills and mindset needed to overcome obstacles and thrive in the face of adversity. Remember challenges are not roadblocks but opportunities for growth and self-improvement.

8

Embracing Individuality

Embracing Individuality is an important aspect of creating a diverse and inclusive society. It involves celebrating and accepting differences among individuals embracing their unique traits and talents breaking gender stereotypes and promoting self-expression and authenticity.

Celebrating Differences:

One way of embracing individuality is by celebrating the differences among people. Each person has their own set of values beliefs perspectives and experiences that shape their identity. By appreciating and respecting these differences we acknowledge the richness and diversity that exists in our society.

For example cultural diversity plays an important role in embracing individuality. Different cultures contribute unique customs traditions and perspectives to society. By recognizing and appreciating these differences we can foster a sense of inclusivity and encourage dialogue and understanding among different cultural groups.

Embracing Unique Traits and Talents:

Another aspect of embracing individuality is recognizing and embracing the unique traits and talents of individuals. Each person possesses a combination of skills abilities and interests that make them unique. By acknowledging and valuing these individual talents we create an environment where everyone feels valued and can contribute their unique strengths.

For instance in the workplace embracing individuality means recognizing and leveraging the diverse skill sets of employees. By encouraging employees to use their unique talents and abilities companies can foster innovation and creativity. This can lead to higher employee satisfaction productivity and ultimately organizational success.

Breaking Gender Stereotypes:

Embracing individuality also involves breaking gender stereotypes. Gender stereotypes are preconceived notions about the roles and behaviors associated with each gender. These stereotypes can limit individuals and hinder their ability to express themselves authentically.

To embrace individuality it is important to challenge and dismantle these stereotypes. For example breaking gender stereotypes means allowing individuals to pursue careers and hobbies that were traditionally associated with the opposite gender. It means encouraging boys to explore their emotions and express vulnerability and girls to pursue careers in male-dominated fields like STEM (science technology engineering and mathematics).

Promoting Self-Expression and Authenticity:

At the heart of embracing individuality is promoting self-expression and authenticity. Each person should feel comfortable being their true self and expressing their thoughts feelings and ideas without fear of judgment or criticism. Encouraging self-expression allows individuals to cultivate their identity and contribute to society in meaningful ways.

For instance promoting self-expression in schools means creating an environment where students are encouraged to express their opinions creativity and individuality. This can be done through art music writing or other modes of self-expression. By providing opportunities for self-expression educators empower students to celebrate their uniqueness and contribute their perspectives to the learning environment.

In addition embracing individuality means supporting individuals who may be marginalized or face discrimination based on their identity. This includes creating inclusive policies and practices that ensure equal opportunities and rights for all individuals regardless of their race gender sexual orientation or other aspects of their identity.

Overall embracing individuality is crucial for creating a diverse and inclusive society. By celebrating differences embracing unique traits and talents breaking gender stereotypes and promoting self-expression and authenticity we create an environment where everyone feels valued and can contribute their unique perspectives and talents. Embracing individuality leads to a more vibrant creative and equitable society.

9

Empowering Others

Empowering others is essential for building a strong society and creating a positive and inclusive environment. It involves providing support opportunities and resources to help others succeed and reach their full potential. In this article we will explore four key aspects of empowering others: being a role model mentoring and supporting others advocating for equality and women's rights and creating opportunities for success.

1. Being a Role Model:
Being a role model means setting a positive example through your own actions behavior and values. By living a life of integrity resilience and empathy you inspire and motivate others to do the same. When you demonstrate your commitment to personal growth and ethical behavior you encourage others to strive for their own improvement.

For instance a successful business leader who prioritizes work-life balance and values employee well-being can inspire their team members to prioritize their own well-being. By openly discussing the importance of self-care setting boundaries and managing stress leaders can show their employees that success does not have to come at the expense of personal health and happiness.

2. Mentoring and Supporting Others:

Mentoring involves offering guidance advice and support to someone who is seeking personal or professional development. As a mentor you share your knowledge expertise and experiences helping others navigate their challenges and achieve their goals.

A mentor can be a trusted friend colleague or coach who shares their wisdom and expertise in a particular area. For example a senior engineer can mentor a junior engineer providing insights on technical skills career development and how to overcome common obstacles in the profession. Through regular meetings constructive feedback and encouragement a mentor can empower their mentee to grow and thrive.

Supporting others can take various forms including emotional support assistance with tasks or projects and fostering a positive and inclusive environment. By offering a helping hand listening attentively and showing empathy and understanding you create a safe and supportive space where others can express themselves and share their concerns.

3. Advocating for Equality and Women's Rights:

Empowering others also involves advocating for equality and women's rights. Gender equality is a fundamental human right and empowering women is crucial for achieving a fair and just society. By speaking out against discrimination championing equal opportunities and challenging societal norms we can create a more inclusive world.

For instance advocating for equal pay is an important step towards achieving gender equality. Women on average earn less than men for performing the same job which perpetuates inequalities in society. By supporting initiatives and policies that ensure equal pay for equal work we can contribute to empowering women and challenging gender-based disparities.

Promoting women's rights also includes advocating against gender-based violence empowering women to participate in decision-making processes and fostering a culture that values diversity and inclusion. By promoting gender equality at all levels of society we can create an environment where everyone has the opportunity to thrive.

4. Creating Opportunities for Success:

One of the crucial aspects of empowering others is creating opportunities for success. This involves recognizing and addressing systemic barriers that prevent certain individuals or groups from accessing resources education and opportunities.

For example in the field of education empowering others includes providing equal educational opportunities regardless of socio-economic background ethnic origin or gender. This can be achieved by offering scholarships mentorship programs and creating inclusive classrooms that value diversity and promote equal participation.

Empowering others also involves creating a supportive and inclusive workplace environment. This can be done by implementing policies and practices that promote diversity and inclusion such as hiring practices that ensure equal opportunities for underrepresented groups providing training on unconscious bias and fostering an inclusive culture that celebrates differences.

Furthermore empowering others can be achieved through entrepreneurship and social initiatives. By creating businesses or organizations that prioritize social impact individuals can contribute to economic development job creation and community empowerment. For example microfinancing programs can empower marginalized individuals especially women to start their own businesses and become financially independent.

In conclusion empowering others is crucial for creating a more equitable and just society. By being a role model mentoring and supporting others advocating for equality and women's rights and creating opportunities for success we can contribute to the positive development and well-being of individuals and communities. Empowering others is a collective effort that requires empathy collaboration and a commitment to social justice.

10

Balancing Attitude with Kindness

Balancing attitude with kindness is an essential trait that fosters healthy relationships effective communication and personal growth. It involves combining resilience assertiveness and a genuine concern for others' well-being. This balance allows individuals to navigate various situations with grace empathy and understanding.

1. Empathy and Compassion:
   Empathy and compassion are the foundations of kindness. Empathy refers to the ability to understand and share the feelings of others while compassion involves taking action to alleviate their suffering. By cultivating empathy we can develop a deeper understanding of different perspectives and appreciate the emotions and experiences of others. When we approach interactions with empathy we can respond to others' needs with kindness and offer support without judgment.

For example imagine a coworker is struggling with work deadlines and appears stressed. Instead of being impatient or dismissive a kind and balanced individual will empathize with their colleague's situation offering assistance or understanding. This approach not only helps build a positive working environment but also enhances productivity and overall well-being.

2. Respecting Others' Perspectives:

Balancing attitude with kindness also means respecting the perspectives and opinions of others even when they differ from our own. It involves open-mindedness and a willingness to engage in meaningful dialogue. By showing respect for diverse viewpoints we can foster an environment of inclusivity and encourage healthy discussions.

For instance consider a situation where a group of individuals is working together to brainstorm ideas for a project. Each member has their own unique perspective and suggestions. A kind and balanced individual will actively listen to each person valuing their input and ensuring that everyone feels heard and respected. This approach not only enhances teamwork but also promotes the development of creative and well-rounded solutions.

3. Constructive Criticism and Feedback:

Balancing attitude with kindness also involves offering constructive criticism and feedback with tact and empathy. Kindness does not mean avoiding criticism altogether but rather providing feedback in a way that is considerate respectful and focused on growth. When criticism is delivered with kindness it becomes an opportunity for learning rather than a source of resentment or defensiveness.

For example in a professional setting a kind and balanced manager will provide feedback to their employees in a supportive and motivating manner. Instead of simply pointing out mistakes or shortcomings they will offer specific suggestions for improvement acknowledging the strengths and efforts of the individual. This approach encourages personal growth fosters a positive work culture and enhances performance.

4. Promoting Unity and Collaboration:

A kind and balanced attitude also encompasses promoting unity and collaboration in all aspects of life. It involves fostering an atmosphere of teamwork cooperation and shared goals. By encouraging inclusivity and valuing the contributions of others we create an environment where everyone feels valued and motivated to work towards a common purpose.

For example a student who demonstrates a balanced attitude will actively engage with their peers fostering a sense of unity within the classroom. They will encourage participation listen to different opinions and seek opportunities for collaborative learning. By promoting unity and collaboration they contribute to a positive academic environment that enhances everyone's learning experiences.

In conclusion balancing attitude with kindness involves incorporating empathy respecting diverse perspectives providing constructive feedback and promoting unity and collaboration. By practicing these principles we cultivate meaningful relationships improve communication and create environments that foster personal and collective growth. Balancing attitude with kindness is not only beneficial to others but also contributes to our own well-being and self-development. Let us strive to embrace this balance in our interactions with others and make a positive difference in the world.

11

Thriving in a Male-Dominated World

In many industries and sectors the world is still predominantly male-dominated. Women often face unique challenges and obstacles in these environments. However it is possible for women to not only survive but thrive in a male-dominated world. In this article we will explore strategies and examples of how women have successfully navigated and excelled in these environments.

1. Challenging Gender Bias:

One of the first steps for women is to challenge and address gender bias. This involves identifying and addressing biased attitudes and behaviors in others as well as self-reflection to identify and overcome any internalized bias. Women can challenge gender bias by speaking up when they witness discrimination advocating for gender equality in the workplace and actively participating in diversity and inclusion initiatives.

For example Sheryl Sandberg the COO of Facebook has been an influential advocate for gender equality and challenging bias in the workplace. She founded the Lean In movement which encourages women to pursue their ambitions and helps them navigate the challenges they face. Sandberg's efforts have inspired countless women to challenge gender bias and strive for success in male-dominated industries.

2. Overcoming Obstacles and Prejudice:

Women in male-dominated industries often face specific obstacles and prejudices that their male counterparts may not experience. These obstacles can include lack of access to opportunities exclusion from networks and mentorship and stereotype threat. To overcome these obstacles women can focus on building their skills seeking out mentors and allies and finding ways to showcase their expertise.

One example is Indra Nooyi the former CEO of PepsiCo. Nooyi faced numerous obstacles as a woman of color in a male-dominated industry. However through her determination strategic thinking and leadership abilities she rose to become one of the most successful and influential businesswomen in the world. Nooyi's journey is a testament to the power of resilience and perseverance in the face of adversity.

3. Building Networks and Allies:

Networking and building professional relationships is crucial for success in any industry but it can be particularly important in male-dominated fields. Women can seek out networks and communities where they can connect with like-minded individuals and receive support. It's also beneficial to cultivate relationships with both men and women who can serve as allies and advocates.

A notable example is Melinda Gates co-founder of the Bill & Melinda Gates Foundation. In her book "The Moment of Lift Gates discusses the importance of building networks and alliances to drive gender equality globally. By engaging with individuals and organizations committed to the cause Gates has leveraged her platform to promote change and empower women in male-dominated societies.

4. Inspiring Change and Progress:

Women who thrive in male-dominated environments also have the power to inspire change and pave the way for future generations. By breaking through barriers and achieving success they become role models and advocates for those who come after them. They can use their platforms to advocate for policies and initiatives that promote gender equality and create more inclusive workplaces.

One influential example is Malala Yousafzai the youngest Nobel Prize laureate. Yousafzai has used her voice and platform to advocate for girls' education and women's rights in male-dominated societies. Her bravery and determination have inspired millions and ignited conversations about the importance of empowering women and creating equal opportunities.

In conclusion thriving in a male-dominated world is not without its challenges but it is undoubtedly possible. Women can challenge gender bias overcome obstacles build networks and allies and inspire change and progress. The examples of influential women like Sheryl Sandberg Indra Nooyi Melinda Gates and Malala Yousafzai demonstrate the power of resilience determination and leadership in breaking through barriers and achieving success in male-dominated industries. By working together and supporting one another women can continue to shape a more inclusive and equal future.

12

Embracing Success with Attitude

Success is a subjective concept that varies from person to person. For some success may mean achieving financial stability while for others it may mean making a positive impact on the world. Regardless of the definition embracing success requires a particular mindset and attitude. In this article we will explore the crucial factors that contribute to embracing success including goal setting and action plans overcoming self-doubt pursuing passion and purpose and celebrating achievements.

Goal Setting and Action Plans:
One of the foundations of embracing success is setting goals and creating action plans to achieve them. Goals provide direction and purpose allowing individuals to focus their efforts and work towards a specific outcome. However setting effective goals requires specific and actionable objectives.

For example suppose someone's goal is to start a successful online business. Instead of having a vague objective like "start a business a more effective approach would be to set specific goals such as "create a business plan within three months "build a website within six months or "reach a customer base of 100 users within one year." These specific goals are measurable time-bound and provide a clear path to success.

Once goals are established creating action plans becomes essential. Action plans outline the steps required to achieve each goal. Breaking down the goals into smaller manageable tasks not only helps individuals stay organized but also increases their chances of success. By taking consistent and focused action individuals can move closer to their desired outcomes ultimately embracing success.

Overcoming Self-Doubt:
Self-doubt is one of the biggest obstacles people face when trying to embrace success. It is the voice in their heads that whispers "You're not good enough or "You'll never achieve your goals." Overcoming self-doubt requires a shift in mindset and the development of self-confidence.

To overcome self-doubt individuals can start by recognizing and challenging their negative thoughts. They can replace self-limiting beliefs with positive affirmations and focus on their strengths and past achievements. It is important to surround themselves with a supportive network of friends family or mentors who can provide encouragement and help build confidence. Seeking professional help such as therapy or coaching can also be beneficial in overcoming self-doubt.

Pursuing Passion and Purpose:
Success is not solely measured by financial gains or external

recognition; it is also about finding fulfillment and happiness. Pursuing passion and purpose plays a vital role in embracing success. When individuals align their goals and actions with their passions and values they are more likely to experience a sense of fulfillment and achieve long-term success.

For instance someone who is passionate about environmental conservation may choose a career in sustainable development or become involved in volunteering for environmental organizations. By pursuing their passion and purpose they not only find personal satisfaction but also make a positive impact in their chosen field. This in turn leads to a more fulfilling and successful life.

Celebrating Achievements:
Celebrating achievements is an essential aspect of embracing success. It not only provides a sense of accomplishment but also motivates individuals to continue striving for their goals. By recognizing and acknowledging their successes individuals become more resilient confident and motivated to achieve even greater heights.

Celebrating achievements can take many forms depending on personal preferences. It could be as simple as treating oneself to a small reward after completing a goal or as significant as organizing a celebration with friends and family after reaching a milestone. The important thing is to take the time to appreciate and reflect on the progress made no matter how small it may seem.

For example if someone set a goal to read 12 books in a year and successfully completed the challenge they could celebrate by taking a day off to relax and indulge in their favorite activities or treat themselves to a new book. By acknowledging their efforts and achievements individuals build a positive mindset and reinforce their commitment to embracing success.

In conclusion embracing success with the right attitude is crucial for personal growth and fulfillment. Setting clear and actionable goals overcoming self-doubt pursuing passions and purpose and celebrating achievements are all essential components of this journey. By adopting these practices individuals can enhance their chances of success and create a life that aligns with their aspirations and values. Remember success is not a destination but a continuous journey of growth and self-discovery.

www.ingramcontent.com/pod-product-compliance
Lightning Source LLC
LaVergne TN
LVHW012128070526
838202LV00056B/5918